QUICK FIX RAMEN NOODLES

101 Simple Recipes

TONI PATRICK

MJF Books
New York

Published by MJF Books
Fine Communications
322 Eighth Avenue
New York, NY 10001

Quick Fix Ramen Noodles
LC Control Number: 2012954100
ISBN-13: 978-1-60671-177-4
ISBN-10: 1-60671-177-6

Consulting Editor: Stephanie Ashcraft
Interior designed by Kurt Wahlner

This book was previously published as *101 Things to Do with Ramen Noodles*

This edition is published by MJF Books in arrangement with Gibbs Smith.

Printed in Malaysia

MJF Books and the MJF colophon are trademarks of Fine Creative Media, Inc.

TWP   10 9 8 7 6 5 4 3 2

This book is dedicated to my
mother. If it weren't for her
threatening to steal my idea
and do the book herself, I
wouldn't have done it.

I love you, Mom,
Toni

CONTENTS

Pork

All-American Ramen 74 • Ham Omelets 75 • Pork Chop Ramen 76 • Cheesy Bacon Noodles 77 • Brats 'n' Noodles 78 • Pork and Peppers 79 • Hungarian Skillet Meal 80 • Lean Pork Steak 81 • Tropical Ramen 82

Seafood

Cheesy Tuna Ramen 84 • Shrimp Ramen 85 • Cheesy Salmon Noodles 86 • Tuna Noodle Casserole 87 • Creamy Mushroom Shrimp Ramen 88 • Twice-Baked Tuna Casserole 89 • Garlic Shrimp 'N' Veggies 90

Family Favorites

Meaty Spaghetti 92 • Cheesy Noodles 93 • Ramen Nachos 94 • Garlic Noodle Saute 95 • Creamy Alfredo Noodles 96 • Mexican Casserole 97 • Pizza Pasta 98 • Lasagna 99 • Primavera Pasta 100 • Beer Noodles 101 • Parmesan Noodles 102 • Cheesy Ranch Ramen 103 • Buttery Chive Noodles 104 • Ramen Trail Mix 105 • Ramen Haystacks 106 • Chocolate Chinos 107 • Peach Treats 108 • Maple and Brown Sugar Ramenmeal 109

Vegetable Entrees

Broccoli-Cauliflower Ramen 112 • Cheesy Vegetable Ramen 113 • Hollandaise Vegetables 114 • Veggie Saute 115 • Chinese Fried Noodles 116 • Tomato Saute 117 • Garlic Cilantro Noodles 118 • Chinese Veggie Noodles 119 • Corny Cheese Noodles 120

HELPFUL HINTS

1. Your freezer is your friend. When buying meat, divide into individual portions and freeze in zipper-lock plastic bags. Buy large bags of frozen vegetables and use portions as needed. Freeze all leftovers—days will come when your pocket is empty or restaurants are closed.

2. When using vegetables, canned, fresh, and frozen are interchangeable. And remember, canned food doesn't spoil until after it has been opened.

3. Macaroni can be used in place of ramen noodles.

4. Save all extra seasoning packets for future use. Sprinkle a seasoning packet over hamburger or chicken and brown together for a great flavor.

5. Macaroni cheese packets can be used in place of real cheese.

6. Two tablespoons dehydrated minced or chopped onion is equal to $1/4$ cup fresh minced onion.

7. Salt lovers beware. Before adding extra salt, taste your food. Seasoning packets are always salty.

8. To cook noodles, follow the directions on the package unless recipe says otherwise.

9. Add more or less of any ingredient to your own liking. Be creative and enjoy yourself.

10. Low-fat or light soups, sour cream, and cream cheese can be substituted if you prefer.

SOUPS

TOMATO NOODLE SOUP

1 package **ramen noodles,** any flavor
1 can (10.75 ounces) **tomato soup,** condensed

Cook noodles in water according to package directions. Do not drain.
Add soup. Simmer 5 minutes, stirring occasionally. Makes 2 servings.

MINESTRONE

1 package	**ramen noodles,** any flavor
1 can (10.75 ounces)	**tomato soup,** condensed
8 ounces	**spicy smoked sausage,** thinly sliced
$^1/_4$ cup	**cooked sliced celery**
$^1/_4$ cup	**cooked sliced carrots**
$^1/_4$ cup	**peas**
$^1/_2$ cup	**green beans**
$^1/_2$ cup	**canned kidney beans,** rinsed and drained
	salt and pepper, to taste

Cook noodles in water according to package directions. Do not drain. Add soup, sausage, and vegetables. Simmer 5–10 minutes, or until vegetables are tender. Add more water by tablespoon if soup is too thick. Season with salt and pepper. Makes 2 servings.

EGG DROP SOUP

2 cups **water**
2 **eggs,** beaten
$^1/_4$ cup **diced onion**
$^1/_4$ cup **diced celery**
$^1/_4$ cup **diced green bell pepper**
1 package **chicken ramen noodles,** with seasoning packet

In a saucepan, bring water to boiling and add seasoning packet, eggs, and vegetables. Stir constantly until eggs look done. Simmer 5 minutes. Add noodles and cook 3–5 minutes more, or until noodles are tender. Makes 2 servings.

BEEFED-UP NOODLES

2 cups	**water**
$1/8$ cup	**diced onion**
$1/8$ cup	**sliced carrots**
$1/8$ cup	**diced celery**
1 sprig	**parsley**
1 small	**bay leaf**
$1/8$ teaspoon	**thyme leaves**
1 package	**beef ramen noodles,** with seasoning packet

In a saucepan, heat all ingredients except noodles and seasoning packet to boiling. Add seasoning packet. Reduce heat and simmer 30 minutes. Strain liquid into a separate container. Add noodles to liquid and cook 3 minutes, or until noodles are done. Makes 2 servings.

CHICKEN CONSOMME AND NOODLES

2 cups	**water**
$1/8$ cup	**diced onion**
$1/8$ cup	**sliced carrots**
$1/8$ cup	**diced celery**
1 sprig	**parsley**
1 small	**bay leaf**
$1/8$ teaspoon	**thyme leaves**
1 package	**chicken ramen noodles,** with seasoning packet

In a saucepan, heat all ingredients except noodles and seasoning packet to boiling. Add seasoning packet. Reduce heat and simmer 30 minutes. Strain liquid into a separate container. Add noodles to liquid and cook 3 minutes, or until noodles are done. Makes 2 servings.

CREAMY MUSHROOM SOUP

I package **ramen noodles,** any flavor
I can (10.75 ounces) **cream of mushroom soup,** condensed
I cup **sliced fresh mushrooms**
salt and pepper, to taste

Cook noodles in water according to package directions and drain.

Prepare soup as directed on can. Mix noodles and soup together. Add mushrooms and simmer 5 minutes. Season with salt and pepper. Makes 2 servings.

CREAMY CHICKEN NOODLE SOUP

1 package **chicken ramen noodles,**
with seasoning packet
1 can (10.75 ounces) **cream of chicken soup,** condensed
$^1/_2$ cup **diced onion**
$^1/_2$ cup **sliced carrots**
$^1/_2$ cup **sliced celery**

Cook noodles in water according to package directions and drain.

Prepare soup as directed on can. Add seasoning packet and vegetables to soup. Cook over medium heat 5–10 minutes, or until vegetables are tender. Add noodles and simmer 2–3 minutes more. Makes 2 servings.

VEGETABLE BEEF NOODLE SOUP

³/4 pound **ground beef**
I cup **chopped tomatoes**
¹/2 cup **chopped carrots**
¹/2 cup **chopped celery**
4 cups **water**
2 packages **beef ramen noodles,** with seasoning packets

In a frying pan, brown and drain beef. Add vegetables, water, and seasoning packets. Bring to a boil and simmer 20 minutes. Add noodles and cook 3 minutes more, or until noodles are done. Makes 2–4 servings.

SUMMER GARDEN SOUP

$^1/_2$ cup	**chopped onion**
1 cup	**julienned zucchini**
$^1/_2$ cup	**chopped carrots**
$^1/_4$ cup	**butter** or **margarine**
1 teaspoon	**basil**
2 packages	**beef ramen noodles,** with seasoning packets
4 cups	**water**
1 cup	**green beans**
1 cup	**chopped tomatoes**

In a frying pan, cook onion, zucchini, and carrots in butter and basil
over medium heat until vegetables are tender.

In a saucepan, combine cooked vegetables, noodles, water, green
beans, tomatoes, and seasoning packets. Bring to boil and simmer
5 minutes. Makes 2–4 servings.

SOUTHWEST VEGETABLE SOUP

I can (10.75 ounces)	**tomato soup,** condensed
I cup	**water**
I can (10 ounces)	**enchilada sauce**
$^1/_2$ cup	**corn**
$^1/_2$ cup	**green beans**
$^1/_2$ cup	**canned kidney beans,** rinsed and drained
$^1/_2$ cup	**salsa**
$^1/_2$ cup	**chopped cooked chicken**
I package	**ramen noodles,** any flavor, crumbled
	tortilla chips
	Monterey Jack cheese, grated

Combine tomato soup, water, and enchilada sauce. Cook over medium heat until hot. Add vegetables, salsa, and chicken. Simmer 15 minutes. Add crumbled noodles and simmer 3–5 minutes more. Serve topped with chips and cheese. Makes 2 servings.

ASIAN BEEF-NOODLE SOUP

I pound	**ground beef,** browned and drained
I	**medium onion,** chopped
I tablespoon	**minced garlic**
I teaspoon	**ground ginger**
5 cups	**water**
I	**medium head bok choy***
2 packages	**beef ramen noodles,** with seasoning packets
I 1/2 teaspoons	**canola oil**
2 tablespoons	**soy sauce**

In a 4-quart soup pan, combine cooked beef, onion, garlic, ginger, and water, and bring to a boil. Stir in bok choy. Simmer over medium heat 3 minutes. Break noodles in half and stir into soup. Simmer 3–5 minutes more, or until noodles are done. Stir in seasoning packets, oil, and soy sauce. Makes 4–6 servings.

*To prepare bok choy for use, rinse with cold water, cut off the very bottom of the stems and discard. Cut remaining bok choy into bite-size pieces.

SALADS

SPRING SALAD

2 packages	**chicken ramen noodles,** with seasoning packets
2 teaspoons	**sesame oil**
3 tablespoons	**lemon juice**
$1/3$ cup	**vegetable oil**
2 teaspoons	**sugar**
I cup	**halved red and/or green seedless grapes**
$1/2$ cup	**diced red and/or green apple**
$1/2$ cup	**diced pineapple chunks**
3 tablespoons	**chopped green onion**
8 ounces	**smoked turkey breast,** cut in strips
$1/4$ cup	**walnut pieces**

Cook noodles in water according to package directions and drain. Rinse with cold water. Add sesame oil and refrigerate.

For dressing, combine lemon juice, vegetable oil, seasoning packets, and sugar. Pour over noodles then add remaining ingredients. Toss to coat. Makes 2–4 servings.

SUMMER PICNIC SALAD

I package **ramen noodles,** any flavor, broken up
$^1/_4$ cup **alfalfa sprouts**
$^1/_2$ cup **peas**
French dressing

Cook noodles in water according to package directions and drain. Top with alfalfa sprouts and peas. Mix with desired amount of dressing. Makes 2 servings.

ZUCCHINI SALAD

I package	**ramen noodles,** any flavor
$^1/_2$ cup	**chopped zucchini**
$^1/_2$ cup	**chopped carrots**
$^1/_8$ cup	**sliced olives**
I teaspoon	**Dijon mustard**
$^1/_2$ teaspoon	**basil**
$^1/_4$ teaspoon	**oregano**
$^1/_4$ teaspoon	**garlic powder**
2 tablespoons	**vinegar**

Cook noodles in water according to package directions and drain. Add vegetables to noodles. Mix together mustard, spices, and vinegar. Add to noodle mixture and toss to coat. Makes 2 servings.

TACO SALAD

2 packages **beef ramen noodles,** with seasoning packets
I pound **ground beef,** browned and drained
I large **tomato,** chopped
$3/4$ cup **chopped onion**
2 cups **grated cheddar cheese**
Thousand Island dressing or **salsa**

Cook noodles in water according to package directions and drain.

In a bowl, stir I seasoning packet into cooked beef. Add tomato, onion, and cheese. Spoon mixture over warm noodles and drizzle with dressing or salsa. Makes 2–4 servings.

THREE-BEAN SALAD

I package **ramen noodles,** any flavor
$^1/_2$ cup **green beans**
$^1/_2$ cup **canned kidney beans,** rinsed and drained
$^1/_2$ cup **canned lima beans,** rinsed and drained
$^1/_4$ cup **Italian dressing**
        salt and pepper, to taste

Cook noodles in water according to package directions and drain. Add beans and stir in dressing. Season with salt and pepper. Makes 2 servings.

ANTIPASTO SALAD

2 packages	**ramen noodles,** any flavor
$3/4$ cup	**cubed pepperoni**
$1/2$ cup	**sliced black olives**
$1/4$ cup	**sliced onion**
	Italian dressing

Cook noodles in water according to package directions and drain. Add pepperoni, olives, and onion. Drizzle desired amount of dressing over top and toss to coat. Makes 2–4 servings.

PASTA SALAD

1 package	**ramen noodles,** any flavor, with seasoning packet
1/2 cup	**mayonnaise**
1 tablespoon	**mustard**
1 1/2 teaspoons	**honey**
1	**celery stalk,** chopped
1/4 cup	**cubed cheddar cheese**
2	**hard-boiled eggs,** chopped

Cook noodles in water according to package directions and drain. Mix mayonnaise, mustard, and honey with 1/2 of the seasoning packet. Add noodles, celery, cheese, and eggs. Toss gently to coat. Makes 2 servings.

ORIENTAL CHICKEN SALAD

1 package **ramen noodles,** any flavor
1 cup **slivered almonds**
1 teaspoon **vinegar**
1/2 cup **oil**
3 teaspoons **seasoned salt**
1/2 teaspoon **pepper**
3 tablespoons **sugar**
4 cups **shredded cooked chicken breast**
3 to 6 **green onions,** sliced
3/4 cup **sliced celery**
1/4 cup **sesame seeds**
1/2 **head lettuce,** torn or shredded

Cook noodles for 1 minute and drain. Roast almonds in oven until lightly browned.

In a bowl, mix vinegar, oil, salt, pepper, and sugar. Add chicken, onions, celery, and sesame seeds. Add lettuce just before serving and toss. Makes 2–4 servings.

FRUITY RAMEN SALAD

Dressing:
- 1/2 teaspoon **salt**
- dash **pepper**
- 1 teaspoon **vegetable oil**
- 1 tablespoon **chopped parsley**
- 2 tablespoons **sugar**
- 2 tablespoons **vinegar**
- dash **Tabasco**

Salad:
- 1 package **ramen noodles,** any flavor
- 1/2 cup **slivered almonds**
- 2 tablespoons **sugar**
- 1 cup **diced fully-cooked ham**
- 1 small can **mandarin oranges,** drained

In a small bowl, combine dressing ingredients and set aside.

Cook noodles in water according to package directions, and then drain and rinse noodles with cold water.

In a frying pan, lightly brown almonds and sugar over medium heat, stirring constantly so almonds are coated in sugar.

In a bowl, mix ham, oranges, and noodles. Add dressing and toss to coat. Just before serving, add almonds and toss again. Makes 2 servings.

WATER CHESTNUT RAMEN SALAD

4 packages	**chicken ramen noodles,** with seasoning packets
I cup	**diced celery**
I can (8 ounces)	**sliced water chestnuts,** drained
I cup	**chopped red onion**
I cup	**diced green bell pepper**
I cup	**peas**
I cup	**mayonnaise**

Break each package of noodles into 4 pieces. Cook noodles in water according to package directions, and then drain and rinse noodles with cold water.

In a large bowl, stir noodles, celery, water chestnuts, onion, pepper, and peas together. Combine mayonnaise and 3 of the 4 seasoning packets. Fold mayonnaise mixture into salad. Cover and refrigerate at least I hour before serving. Makes 4–6 servings.

SWEET-AND-SOUR SALAD

I cup	**canola** or **olive oil**
1/2 cup	**sugar**
1/2 cup	**cider vinegar**
I tablespoon	**soy sauce**
1/2 cup	**butter**
I cup	**chopped walnuts**
I package	**ramen noodles,** any flavor, crushed
I head	**romaine lettuce**
4 cups	**chopped fresh broccoli**
1/2 cup	**chopped green onions**

Combine oil, sugar, vinegar, and soy sauce together and refrigerate overnight.

In a saucepan, melt butter over medium heat. Stir walnuts and noodles into butter. Stir until heated.

Tear lettuce into bite-size pieces and place in a large bowl. Add broccoli and onions. Pour dressing over top and toss to coat. Sprinkle walnuts and ramen mixture over salad. Makes 6–8 servings.

BEEF

BEEF RAMENOFF

¹/₂ pound	**beef strips**
2 cups	**sour cream**
I tablespoon	**chopped chives**
I teaspoon	**salt**
¹/₈ teaspoon	**pepper**
I	**garlic clove,** crushed
¹/₂ cup	**grated Parmesan cheese,** divided
I packages	**ramen noodles,** any flavor
2 tablespoons	**butter** or **margarine**

In a frying pan, brown beef until done. Add sour cream, spices, and ¹/₄ cup Parmesan and simmer over low heat.

Cook noodles in water according to package directions and drain. Stir butter into warm noodles until melted. Fold in beef mixture. Sprinkle with reserved cheese. Makes 2 servings.

CHEESEBURGER RAMEN

$^1/_2$ pound **ground beef**
1 package **beef ramen noodles,** with seasoning packet
1 cup **grated cheddar cheese**
1 **tomato,** diced (optional)

In a frying pan, brown and drain beef. Season to taste with $^1/_2$ of the seasoning packet.

Cook noodles in water according to package directions and drain. Add beef and cheese to noodles and stir until cheese is melted. Add tomatoes, if desired. Makes 2 servings.

CREAMY BEEF AND BROCCOLI NOODLES

$^3/_4$ pound **beef sirloin,** cubed
$^1/_2$ teaspoon **garlic powder**
1 **onion,** cut in wedges
2 cups **broccoli pieces**
1 can (10.75 ounces) **cream of broccoli soup,** condensed
$^1/_4$ cup **water**
1 tablespoon **soy sauce**
2 packages **beef ramen noodles,**
with seasoning packets

In a frying pan, brown beef with garlic powder until done. Stir in onion and broccoli. Cook over medium heat until vegetables are tender. Add soup, water, and soy sauce. Simmer 10 minutes.

Cook noodles in water according to package directions and drain. Add seasoning packets. Serve beef mixture over warm noodles. Makes 2 servings.

BEEF PROVENCALE

1 pound **beef strips**
2 tablespoons **butter** or **margarine**
1 **onion,** sliced
2 tablespoons **flour**
1 cup **water mixed with seasoning packet**
1 **tomato,** chopped
1 can (4 ounces) **sliced mushrooms,** drained
1 teaspoon **garlic powder**
1 package **beef ramen noodles,** with seasoning packet

In a frying pan, brown beef until done.

In a saucepan, heat butter until golden brown. Add onion and cook until tender, then discard onion. Stir in flour, over low heat, until it is brown. Remove from heat. Add water mixture and heat to boiling, stirring constantly for 1 minute. Gently stir in tomato, mushrooms, and garlic powder.

Cook noodles in water according to package directions and drain. Top warm noodles with beef and sauce. Makes 2 servings.

MARINATED BEEF

3/4 pound	**beef strips**
I package	**beef ramen noodles,** with seasoning packet
1/2 cup	**water**
2 tablespoons	**oil**
1/4 cup	**sliced green onion**
I tablespoon	**butter** or **margarine**
I can (14.5 ounces)	**diced tomatoes,** drained

Marinate beef in seasoning packet, water, and oil for 30 minutes. Cook beef in marinade until done. Add onion and butter, and saute 5 minutes.

Cook noodles in water according to package directions and drain. Add tomatoes and cooked noodles to beef mixture. Simmer 5–10 minutes, or until heated through. Makes 2 servings.

CHEDDAR BEEF CASSEROLE

2 packages	**beef ramen noodles,** with seasoning packets
I pound	**ground beef**
$^1/_2$ cup	**sliced celery**
$^1/_4$ cup	**chopped green bell pepper**
$^1/_2$ cup	**chopped onion**
3 cups	**grated cheddar cheese**
2 cups	**corn**
I can (6 ounces)	**tomato paste**
$^1/_2$ cup	**water**

Preheat oven to 350 degrees.

Cook noodles in water according to package directions; drain and set aside.

In a frying pan, brown beef with celery, pepper, and onion. Set aside.

In a 2-quart casserole dish, mix remaining ingredients with I seasoning packet. Add beef mixture and noodles. Bake 15–20 minutes. Makes 2–4 servings.

BEEF AND BROCCOLI STIR-FRY

I pound **beef steak strips**
I tablespoon **oil**
2 cups **broccoli pieces**
I cup **green onions,** cut in strips
2 tablespoons **soy sauce**
$1/4$ teaspoon **crushed red pepper**
2 packages **beef ramen noodles,** with seasoning packets

In a frying pan, brown and drain beef. Add oil, I seasoning packet, broccoli, and onions. Stir-fry 5 minutes. Add soy sauce and red pepper. Simmer 5 minutes more.

Cook noodles in water according to package directions and drain. Serve beef mixture over warm noodles. Makes 2–4 servings.

BEEFY MUSHROOM NOODLES

2 packages	**beef ramen noodles,** with seasoning packets
1 1/2 pounds	**beef strips**
1/4 cup	**butter** or **margarine**
2 cans (4 ounces each)	**sliced mushrooms,** drained
1/4 cup	**flour**
2 cups	**water mixed with seasoning packets**
	Worcestershire sauce

Cook noodles in water according to package directions and drain.

In a frying pan, brown and drain beef until done.

In a small saucepan, melt butter over low heat. Stir in mushrooms and brown slowly. Add flour and cook, stirring, until deep brown. Add water mixture. Heat to boiling and stir 1 minute. Add Worcestershire sauce to taste. Top warm noodles with beef and sauce. Makes 2–4 servings.

BEEF SUKIYAKI

I pound **stir-fry beef**
2 tablespoons **oil**
$^1/_2$ cup **water mixed with half of seasoning packet**
2 tablespoons **sugar**
$^1/_2$ cup **soy sauce**
I can (4 ounces) **sliced mushrooms,** drained
$^1/_2$ cup **sliced green onions**
I cup **sliced onion**
I **celery stalk,** sliced
I small can **bamboo shoots**
3 cups **fresh spinach**
2 packages **beef ramen noodles,** with seasoning packets

In a frying pan, brown beef in oil until done, and then push to one side of the pan. Stir in water, sugar, and soy sauce. Add remaining ingredients except noodles and cook until tender. Cover and simmer 5 minutes. Stir together.

Cook noodles in water according to package directions and drain. Add seasoning packets. Serve beef mixture over warm noodles. Makes 2–4 servings.

VEGETABLE BEEF NOODLES

¹/2 pound **ground beef**
I can (8 ounces) **tomato sauce**
2 cups **frozen mixed vegetables**
I package **beef ramen noodles,** with seasoning packet

In a frying pan, brown and drain beef. Add tomato sauce, seasoning packet, and vegetables to cooked beef. Simmer 10 minutes, or until vegetables are tender.

Cook noodles in water according to package directions and drain. Add noodles to beef mixture and simmer 2–3 minutes. Makes 2 servings.

BEEF 'N' POTATO NOODLES

    1 pound **ground beef**
     2 cups **cubed potatoes**
     2 cups **diced tomatoes**
  2 packages **beef ramen noodles,** with seasoning packets

In a frying pan, brown beef with seasoning packets until done. Add potatoes and cook until tender.

Cook noodles in water according to package directions and drain. Stir in tomatoes, then add noodles and tomatoes to beef mixture and simmer 5 minutes. Makes 2–4 servings.

BEEFY CHILI NOODLES

I pound **ground beef**
2 packages **beef ramen noodles,**
with seasoning packets
2 cans (4 ounces each) **sliced mushrooms,** drained
$^1/_2$ cup **chopped onion**
$^1/_2$ cup **chopped tomato**
I can (15 ounces) **kidney beans,** rinsed and drained
$^1/_4$ teaspoon **chili powder**
I cup **water**

In a frying pan, brown and drain beef. Add remaining ingredients and
I seasoning packet. Simmer 10 minutes over medium heat or until
noodles are done. Makes 2–4 servings.

RAMEN BURGERS

1 package	**beef ramen noodles,** with seasoning packet
1 pound	**ground beef**
1	**egg**
	hamburger buns
	condiments

Cook noodles 1 1/2 minutes and drain. Add beef, egg, and 1/2 of the seasoning packet. Mix well and form into four patties. Grill or cook 5 minutes per side, or until done. Serve with the usual hamburger fixings. Makes 4 hamburgers.

SPICY BEEF NOODLES

2 packages	**ramen noodles,** any flavor, with seasoning packets
$1/2$ pound	**ground beef**
$1/2$ pound	**ground spicy sausage**
$1/2$ cup	**diced onion**
$3/4$ cup	**diced green bell pepper**
$3/4$ cup	**salsa**

Cook noodles in water according to package directions; drain and set aside.

In a frying pan, brown and drain beef and sausage together. Add onion, pepper, and salsa. Cook until vegetables are tender; add noodles and simmer 2–3 minutes. Makes 2–4 servings.

SPICY MEAT LOAF CHEESE ROLL

I pound **ground beef**
I package **beef ramen noodles,** crushed
I cup **grated cheddar cheese**
$^1/_2$ cup **salsa**

Preheat oven to 350 degrees.

Flatten beef into a $^1/_2$-inch-thick rectangle. Sprinkle uncooked noodles over beef. Top with a layer of cheese. Roll from one end to the other and pinch ends to prevent cheese from melting to the outside. Top with salsa. Bake 30 minutes. Top with more salsa before serving, if desired. Makes 2–4 servings.

COUNTRY VEGETABLE BEEF

2 cups **water**
2 tablespoons **cornstarch**
I pound **ground beef**
4 cups **frozen mixed vegetables**
2 packages **beef ramen noodles,** with seasoning packets

In a small saucepan, mix water, cornstarch, and seasoning packets. Stir constantly over low heat until mixture thickens.

In a frying pan, brown and drain beef. Add vegetables and cook until tender. Add gravy and stir.

Cook noodles in water according to package directions and drain. Serve beefy gravy over warm noodles. Makes 2–4 servings.

BEEFY NOODLES WITH GRAVY

1 pound **beef strips**
1 package **beef ramen noodles,** with seasoning packet
1 envelope **brown gravy**

In a frying pan, brown beef until done.

Cook noodles in water according to package directions; drain and set aside.

In a saucepan, cook gravy according to package directions. Top warm noodles with beef and gravy. Makes 2 servings.

CHICKEN

CREAMY CHICKEN
AND BROCCOLI

3 **boneless, skinless chicken breasts,** cut into strips
2 cups **cut-up fresh** or **frozen broccoli**
2 cans (10.75 ounces each) **cream of mushroom soup,** condensed
$^1/_2$ cup water
2 packages **chicken ramen noodles,** with seasoning packets

In a frying pan, brown chicken until done. Add broccoli and soup to chicken; cook over medium heat until broccoli is tender. Add $^1/_2$ of 1 seasoning packet, or to taste.

Cook noodles in water according to package directions and drain. Serve chicken and broccoli mixture over warm noodles. Makes 2–4 servings.

SPICY CHICKEN

3 **boneless, skinless chicken breasts,** cut into strips
³/₄ teaspoon **garlic powder**
1 can (14.5 ounces) **diced tomatoes with green chiles,** drained
1 cup **chopped green bell peppers**
2 cups **water**
2 packages **chicken ramen noodles,** with seasoning packets

In a frying pan, brown chicken until done. Add garlic powder, tomatoes, peppers, water, and seasoning packets. Simmer 10 minutes. Add noodles and cook 3–5 minutes more. Makes 2–4 servings.

CHEESY CHICKEN DIVAN

2 cups	**fresh broccoli pieces**
2 to 4	**boneless, skinless chicken breasts,** cut into chunks
2 packages	**chicken ramen noodles**
I can (10.75 ounces)	**cream of chicken soup,** condensed
³/₄ cup	**mayonnaise**
I teaspoon	**mild curry powder**
	salt and pepper, to taste
I cup	**grated cheddar cheese**

Preheat oven to 350 degrees.

Place broccoli in a saucepan and cover with water. Cook over medium heat until broccoli is tender; drain and spread in a lightly greased 9 x 9-inch casserole dish.

In a frying pan, brown chicken until done. Spread chicken over broccoli.

Cook noodles in water according to package directions and drain. Spread noodles over broccoli and chicken.

Mix together soup, mayonnaise, curry powder, salt, and pepper. Spoon mixture over broccoli, chicken, and noodles; sprinkle with cheese and bake 30 minutes. Makes 2–4 servings.

CHICKEN LO MEIN

I tablespoon **oil**
I tablespoon **soy sauce**
I pound **boneless, skinless chicken breasts,**
            cut into strips
$1/2$ cup **sliced onion**
$1/2$ cup **chopped green bell pepper**
$1/4$ cup **chopped carrot**
I package **chicken ramen noodles,** with seasoning packet

In a frying pan, mix oil, soy sauce, and $1/2$ of the seasoning packet. Add chicken and brown until done. Add vegetables to chicken, and cook until tender.

Cook noodles in water according to package directions and drain. Add noodles to chicken and vegetables and cook over medium heat 3 minutes, stirring constantly. Makes 2 servings.

CHICKEN HOLLANDAISE

2 to 4 **boneless, skinless chicken breasts,**
cut into chunks

4 **egg yolks**

6 tablespoons **lemon juice**

I cup **butter** or **margarine,** divided

2 packages **chicken ramen noodles,**
with seasoning packets

In a frying pan, brown chicken until done. Season with $^1/_2$ of I seasoning packet, or to taste.

In a small saucepan, whisk egg yolks and lemon juice briskly with a fork. Add $^1/_2$ cup butter and stir over low heat until melted. Add remaining butter, stirring briskly until butter melts and sauce thickens.

Cook noodles in water according to package directions and drain. Top warm noodles with chicken and sauce. Makes 2–4 servings.

CHICKEN VELOUTE

I pound	**boneless, skinless chicken breasts,** cut into chunks
2 tablespoons	**butter** or **margarine**
2 tablespoons	**flour**
I cup	**water mixed with seasoning packet**
1/8 teaspoon	**nutmeg**
I package	**chicken ramen noodles,** with seasoning packet

In a frying pan, brown chicken until done.

In a saucepan, melt butter over low heat. Mix in flour, stirring until smooth and bubbly. Remove from heat. Stir in water mixture and nutmeg. Heat to boiling, stirring I minute. Add chicken and simmer over low heat.

Cook noodles in water according to package directions and drain. Top warm noodles with chicken and sauce. Makes 2 servings.

CHICKEN CURRY

                     2 **boneless, skinless chicken breasts**
              $1/4$ cup **butter** or **margarine**
              $1/4$ cup **flour**
         $1/2$ teaspoon **curry powder**
               2 cups **milk**
           2 packages **chicken ramen noodles,**
                        with seasoning packets

In a frying pan, brown chicken until done. Set aside.

In a small saucepan, melt butter. Stir in flour, curry powder, and I seasoning packet. Cook on low heat, stirring until smooth and bubbly. Add milk and heat to boiling, stirring I minute. Add chicken and simmer over low heat.

Cook noodles in water according to package directions and drain. Top warm noodles with chicken and sauce. Makes 2 servings.

CHICKEN DIABLO

2	**boneless, skinless chicken breasts,** cut into chunks
I package	**chicken ramen noodles,** with seasoning packet
2 tablespoons	**butter** or **margarine**
2 tablespoons	**flour**
I cup	**water mixed with seasoning packet**
2 tablespoons	**chopped onion**
I tablespoon	**vinegar**
I tablespoon	**chopped parsley**
$^1/_4$ teaspoon	**tarragon leaves**
$^1/_4$ teaspoon	**thyme leaves**

In a frying pan, brown chicken until done. Cook noodles in water according to package directions; drain and set aside.

In a small saucepan, heat butter over low heat until golden brown. Blend in flour, stirring until deep brown. Remove from heat. Add water mixture, onion, vinegar, and herbs, and heat to boiling, stirring I minute. Top warm noodles with chicken and sauce. Makes 2 servings.

CREAMY CHICKEN NOODLES

I package **chicken ramen noodles,**
with seasoning packet
I can (10.75 ounces) **cream of chicken soup,** condensed
$^1/_4$ cup **diced onion**
I small can **chicken**

Cook noodles in water according to package directions and drain.

In a saucepan, heat soup, onion, chicken, and just under $^1/_2$ of the seasoning packet, over medium heat 5 minutes. Top warm noodles with soup mixture. Makes 2 servings.

CHICKEN WITH MUSHROOMS

$^1/_4$ cup **butter** or **margarine**
I pound **boneless, skinless chicken tenders,**
cut into chunks
2 cups **sliced fresh mushrooms**
2 packages **chicken ramen noodles,**
with seasoning packets

In a frying pan, melt butter and brown chicken until done. Add mushrooms and saute 5 minutes, or until tender.

Cook noodles in water according to package directions and drain. Add I seasoning packet. Top warm noodles with chicken and mushrooms. Makes 2–4 servings.

CHICKEN ALLEMANDE

2 **boneless, skinless chicken breasts,** cut into chunks

2 packages **chicken ramen noodles,** with seasoning packets

2 tablespoons **flour**

salt and pepper, to taste

1/8 teaspoon **nutmeg**

1 **egg yolk**

1 cup **water mixed with 1 seasoning packet**

2 tablespoons **butter** or **margarine,** melted

2 tablespoons **cream**

1 teaspoon **lemon juice**

In a frying pan, brown chicken until done.

Cook noodles in water according to package directions and drain.

In a saucepan, mix flour, salt, pepper, and nutmeg together. Beat egg yolk and water mixture together, and then stir into flour mixture. Heat to boiling and boil 1 minute, stirring constantly. Remove from heat. Stir in butter, cream, and lemon juice. Add chicken and simmer 2–3 minutes. Top warm noodles with chicken and sauce. Makes 2 servings.

CHICKEN ALFREDO

2 **boneless, skinless chicken breasts,** cut in strips
2 packages **ramen noodles,** any flavor
1 cup **butter** or **margarine**
1 cup **cream**
2 cups **grated Parmesan cheese**
2 tablespoons **parsley flakes**
1/2 teaspoon **salt**
pepper

In a frying pan, brown chicken until done.

Cook noodles in water according to package directions and drain.

Heat butter and cream in a small saucepan over low heat until butter melts. Stir in remaining ingredients. Keep warm over low heat. Top warm noodles with chicken and sauce. Makes 2 servings.

RAMEN FAJITAS

2	**boneless, skinless chicken breasts,** cut in strips
1 1/2 cups	**sliced onion**
1 cup	**sliced red** or **green bell peppers**
2 cups	**salsa**
2 packages	**ramen noodles,** any flavor
1/2 cup	**sour cream**

In a frying pan, brown chicken until done. Add onion, peppers, and salsa and cook over medium heat until vegetables are tender.

Cook noodles in water according to package directions and drain. Serve chicken mixture over warm noodles and top with sour cream. Makes 2 servings.

ITALIAN CHICKEN

2 packages **ramen noodles,** any flavor
2 **boneless, skinless chicken breasts,** cut into chunks
I cup **Italian dressing,** divided

Cook noodles in water according to package directions and drain. If possible, let chicken marinate overnight in $1/2$ cup dressing.

In a frying pan, cook chicken in the dressing until golden brown. Drizzle remaining dressing on noodles and toss. Top with chicken. Makes 2 servings.

FIESTA CHICKEN

I pound	**boneless, skinless chicken breasts,** cut into chunks
	olive oil
¹/₂ cup	**corn**
¹/₂ cup	**black beans,** drained and rinsed
¹/₂ cup	**chopped red bell pepper**
2 packages	**cajun chicken ramen noodles,** with seasoning packets
2 to 3 tablespoons	**sour cream**
2 tablespoons	**salsa**

In a frying pan, brown chicken in olive oil. Add corn, black beans, and pepper. Saute over low heat until heated through and vegetables are tender.

Cook noodles in water according to package directions and drain. Add seasoning packets. Combine noodles with chicken mixture. Stir in sour cream and salsa. Makes 2–4 servings.

CHEESY CHICKEN CASSEROLE

$^1/_4$ cup **chopped onion**
2 tablespoons **butter** or **margarine**
1 can (10.75 ounces) **cream of chicken soup,** condensed
$^1/_2$ cup **milk**
1 package **chicken ramen noodles,**
with seasoning packet
1 cup **grated sharp cheddar cheese**
1 small can **white chicken chunks,** drained

Preheat oven to 350 degrees.

In a saucepan, saute onion in butter until tender. Add soup, milk, and just under $^1/_2$ of the seasoning packet. Stir until smooth.

Cook noodles in water according to package directions and drain. Add cheese, chicken, and soup mixture. Stir until cheese is melted. Pour into a 1-quart greased casserole dish and bake 30 minutes. Makes 2 servings.

CHICKEN 'N' ASPARAGUS

4	**boneless, skinless chicken breasts**
2 packages	**chicken ramen noodles,** with seasoning packets
2 cans (10.75 ounces each)	**cream of asparagus** or **mushroom soup,** condensed
1 cup	**milk**
1/2 pound	**fresh asparagus,** cut up
1 cup	**grated cheddar cheese**

In a frying pan, brown chicken until done. Add remaining ingredients, except cheese and 1 seasoning packet. Simmer over low heat 10 minutes, or until noodles are done. Sprinkle with cheese before serving. Makes 4 servings.

CHINESE-STYLE RAMEN

1/2 pound	**boneless, skinless chicken breasts,** cut into chunks
1/4 cup	**water chestnut halves**
1/2 cup	**snow peas**
1/3 cup	**bean sprouts**
1/4 cup	**celery**
2 to 3 teaspoons	**oil**
I package	**Oriental ramen noodles,** with seasoning packet
I tablespoon	**soy sauce**

In a frying pan, brown chicken until done. Add water chestnuts, snow peas, bean sprouts, celery, and oil. Saute until vegetables are tender.

Cook noodles in water according to package directions and drain. Add seasoning packet. Spoon vegetables over warm noodles and sprinkle with soy sauce. Makes 2 servings.

CHICKEN MILANO

1 pound	**boneless, skinless chicken breasts,** cut into chunks
2 teaspoons	**minced garlic**
1 tablespoon	**olive oil**
1/2 cup	**chopped sun-dried tomatoes**
1 tablespoon	**basil**
1/2 cup	**chicken broth**
2 packages	**chicken ramen noodles,** with seasoning packets
	salt and pepper, to taste

In a frying pan, brown chicken and garlic in oil until done. Add sun-dried tomatoes, basil, and chicken broth. Simmer over low heat 5 minutes.

Cook noodles in water according to package directions and drain. Add 1 seasoning packet. Serve chicken mixture over warm noodles. Season with salt and pepper. Makes 2–4 servings.

PORK

ALL-AMERICAN RAMEN

2 packages **ramen noodles,** any flavor, with seasoning packets
$^1/_4$ cup **chopped onion**
4 **hot dogs,** sliced
1 cup **grated cheddar cheese**

Cook noodles in water according to package directions and drain. Add seasoning packets.

In a frying pan, saute onion and hot dogs together until heated through. Add hot dog mixture to noodles. Add cheese and stir until melted. Makes 2–4 servings.

HAM OMELETS

2 packages **ramen noodles,** any flavor, with seasoning packets
2 tablespoons **butter** or **margarine**
6 **eggs,** beaten
I cup **chopped ham**
$^1/_2$ cup **chopped onion**
$^1/_2$ cup **chopped green bell pepper**
$^1/_2$ to I cup **grated Swiss cheese**

Cook noodles in water according to package directions and drain. Add seasoning packets.

In a frying pan, melt butter, and then add beaten eggs. Fold in noodles and remaining ingredients. Cook until light brown. Makes 2–4 servings.

PORK CHOP RAMEN

4 **pork chops**
1 teaspoon **oil**
$^1/_2$ cup **sliced onion**
1 can (10.75 ounces) **cream of celery soup,** condensed
$^1/_2$ cup **water**
2 packages **pork ramen noodles,**
with seasoning packets

In a frying pan over medium heat, brown pork chops in oil 5 minutes per side, or until done, and drain. Add onion, soup, and water. Simmer over low heat 10 minutes.

Cook noodles in water according to package directions and drain. Add seasoning packets. Serve pork chops and sauce over warm noodles. Makes 4 servings.

CHEESY BACON NOODLES

2 packages	**ramen noodles,** any flavor
2 cups	**grated cheddar cheese**
$^1/_2$ to 1 cup	**bacon,** cooked and crumbled
	salt and pepper, to taste

Cook noodles in water according to package directions and drain. Add cheese immediately and stir until melted. Stir in bacon and season with salt and pepper. Makes 2–4 servings.

BRATS 'N' NOODLES

2 packages **ramen noodles,** any flavor, with seasoning packets
4 **bratwursts** or **cheddarwursts,** sliced

Boil noodles and brats together. Drain and stir in 1 seasoning packet.
Makes 2–4 servings.

PORK AND PEPPERS

2	**pork chops**
$1/4$ cup	**chopped red bell pepper**
$1/4$ cup	**chopped green bell pepper**
2 tablespoons	**chopped onion**
1 package	**pork ramen noodles,** with seasoning packet
2 tablespoons	**butter** or **margarine**
2 tablespoons	**flour**
1 cup	**water mixed with seasoning packet**
1 tablespoon	**vinegar**
$1/4$ teaspoon	**tarragon leaves**
$1/4$ teaspoon	**thyme leaves**

In a frying pan, brown pork chops until done and then remove. Saute peppers and onion in drippings until tender.

Cook noodles in water according to package directions and drain.

In a small saucepan, heat butter over low heat until light brown. Add flour, stirring until deep brown. Remove from heat. Add remaining ingredients. Heat to boiling and stir 1 minute. Top warm noodles with pork chops and sauce. Makes 2 servings.

HUNGARIAN SKILLET MEAL

I package **ramen noodles,** any flavor
$^1/_2$ pound **pork strips**
I can (8 ounces) **tomato sauce**
$^1/_4$ cup **onion,** thinly sliced
I teaspoon **paprika**
$^1/_3$ cup **sour cream**

Cook noodles in water according to package directions and drain.

In a frying pan, brown pork until done. Add tomato sauce, onion, paprika, and noodles. Cook over low heat until onion is tender. Stir in noodles. Remove from heat and add sour cream. Makes 2 servings.

LEAN PORK STEAK

2 packages **pork ramen noodles,** with seasoning packets
2 **lean pork steaks,** cut into bite-size pieces
1 teaspoon **dried minced onion**
$^3/_4$ cup **water**

Cook noodles in water according to package directions and drain.

In a frying pan, cook steak pieces until done. Add onion, water, and seasoning packets. Simmer, covered, 10 minutes. Stir in noodles and simmer 3–5 minutes more. Makes 2 servings.

TROPICAL RAMEN

2 packages **ramen noodles,** any flavor
2 cups **fully-cooked ham,** cut in strips
1 cup **pineapple chunks**
1 cup **crispy Chinese noodles**
1 stalk **celery,** sliced

Cook noodles in water according to package directions and drain. Rinse with cold water.

Stir in ham, pineapple, crispy noodles, and celery. Makes 2 servings.

SEAFOOD

CHEESY TUNA RAMEN

2 packages	**ramen noodles,** any flavor
2 cans (10.75 ounces each)	**cream of mushroom soup,** condensed
1 cup	**milk**
2 cans	**tuna,** drained
2 cups	**peas**
2 cups	**grated cheddar cheese**

Cook noodles in water according to package directions and drain. Add soup, milk, tuna, and peas. Simmer 5 minutes. Sprinkle cheese over top and serve. Makes 2–4 servings.

SHRIMP RAMEN

1 package **Oriental ramen noodles,**
with seasoning packet
1 can (10.75 ounces) **cream of celery soup,** condensed
1 can **shrimp,** drained
salt and pepper, to taste

Cook noodles in water according to package directions and drain. Add just under $1/2$ of the seasoning packet. Add soup, shrimp, salt, and pepper. Cook 10 minutes over medium heat. Makes 2 servings.

CHEESY SALMON NOODLES

1 package	**ramen noodles,** any flavor
1 can (10.75 ounces)	**cream of mushroom soup,** condensed
1/2 cup	**milk**
1 small can	**salmon,** drained
1 cup	**cooked spinach** or **asparagus**
1 cup	**grated cheddar cheese**

Cook noodles in water according to package directions and drain. Add soup, milk, salmon, and broccoli. Simmer 5 minutes. Sprinkle cheese over top and serve. Makes 2 servings.

TUNA NOODLE CASSEROLE

2 cans **tuna,** drained
1 cup **grated cheddar cheese**
$^1/_2$ cup **water**
1 cup **milk**
2 **eggs,** beaten
2 packages **chicken ramen noodles,** broken up,
with seasoning packets
10 to 20 **saltine crackers,** crushed

Preheat oven to 350 degrees.

In a bowl, mix tuna, cheese, water, milk, eggs, and 1 seasoning packet.
Transfer mixture to a casserole dish. Add broken uncooked noodles.
Bake 15 minutes, stirring occasionally. Sprinkle crackers over top and
bake 5 minutes more. Makes 2–4 servings.

CREAMY MUSHROOM SHRIMP RAMEN

I package **Oriental ramen noodles,**
with seasoning packet
I can (10.75 ounces) **cream of mushroom soup,** condensed
I can **shrimp,** drained
I cup **sliced fresh mushrooms**

Cook noodles in water according to package directions; do not drain.
Add soup, shrimp, mushrooms, and $1/2$ of the seasoning packet. Cook
10 minutes over medium heat. Makes 2 servings.

TWICE-BAKED TUNA CASSEROLE

2 packages **ramen noodles,** any flavor, with seasoning packets
2 cans **tuna,** drained
1 cup **cheese**
$^1/_2$ cup **chopped onion**
1 cup **crushed potato chips**

Preheat oven to 350 degrees.

Cook noodles in water according to package directions and drain. Season with 1 seasoning packet. Mix tuna, cheese, onion, and noodles together in a small casserole dish and bake 15–20 minutes. Sprinkle chips over top and bake 15 minutes more. Makes 2–4 servings.

GARLIC SHRIMP 'N' VEGGIES

1	**green bell pepper,** thinly sliced
1	**red bell pepper,** thinly sliced
1/2	**small onion,** thinly sliced
1 1/2 tablespoons	**minced garlic**
3 to 4 tablespoons	**olive oil**
2 cups	**cooked small shrimp,** peeled and deveined
2 packages	**Oriental ramen noodles,** with seasoning packets

In a frying pan, saute peppers, onion, and garlic in olive oil until tender. Add shrimp and 1 seasoning packet. Simmer 3–5 minutes.

Cook noodles in water according to package directions and drain. Add 1/2 of remaining seasoning packet. Serve shrimp mixture over noodles. Makes 2–4 servings.

Family Favorites

MEATY SPAGHETTI

2 packages **ramen noodles,** any flavor
I to 2 cups **spaghetti sauce**
I pound **ground beef** or **sausage,** browned and drained
grated Parmesan cheese

Cook noodles in water according to package directions and drain.

In a saucepan, heat sauce and cooked beef over medium heat 3–5 minutes, or until heated through. Spoon sauce over warm noodles and then sprinkle with cheese. Makes 2–4 servings.

CHEESY NOODLES

2 packages **ramen noodles,** any flavor
1 cup **cubed American processed cheese**
$^{1}/_{2}$ to $^{3}/_{4}$ cup **milk**
salt and pepper, to taste

Cook noodles in water according to package directions and drain. Add cheese and milk and stir until cheese is melted. Season with salt and pepper. Makes 2–4 servings.

RAMEN NACHOS

1 package **beef ramen noodles,** broken up,
with seasoning packet
$^1/_2$ cup **cubed American processed cheese**
1 cup **chili**
1 cup **crushed corn chips**
sour cream
green onion, chopped

Cook noodles in water according to package directions and drain. Add
$^1/_2$ of the seasoning packet.

In a saucepan, stir warm noodles, cheese, chili, and crushed chips
together over low heat until cheese is melted. Garnish with sour cream
and green onion. Makes 2 servings.

GARLIC NOODLE SAUTE

2 packages	**chicken ramen noodles,** with seasoning packets
2 cups	**sliced fresh mushrooms**
$^1/_2$	**red onion,** sliced
I tablespoon	**minced garlic**
	olive oil

Cook noodles in water according to package directions and drain. Season with I seasoning packet.

In a frying pan, saute mushrooms, onion, and garlic in olive oil until tender. Add warm noodles and saute 2 minutes. Makes 2–4 servings.

CREAMY ALFREDO NOODLES

2 packages	**ramen noodles,** any flavor
1 cup	**butter** or **margarine**
1 cup	**cream**
2 cups	**freshly grated Parmesan cheese**
1 teaspoon	**garlic salt**
	Italian seasoning, to taste
	pepper, to taste

Cook noodles in water according to package directions and drain.

In a saucepan, heat butter and cream over low heat until butter is melted. Stir in remaining ingredients. Simmer sauce 5 minutes. Serve sauce over warm noodles. Makes 2–3 servings.

MEXICAN CASSEROLE

2 packages **chicken mushroom ramen noodles,**
with seasoning packets
1 cup **cubed Monterey Jack cheese**
$^1/_2$ cup **diced green chiles**
$^1/_4$ cup **sliced black olives**
1 cup **sour cream**
1 cup **grated cheddar cheese**
$^1/_4$ cup **grated Parmesan cheese**
$^1/_2$ cup **crushed corn chips**

Preheat oven to 400 degrees.

Cook noodles in water according to package directions; rinse with cold water. Combine noodles, seasoning packets, Monterey Jack cheese, chiles, and olives. Stir in sour cream. Spoon noodle mixture into a greased casserole dish. Sprinkle with remaining cheeses and chips. Bake 20 minutes, or until brown and bubbly. Makes 2–4 servings.

PIZZA PASTA

2 packages **ramen noodles,** any flavor
2 to 3 cups **spaghetti sauce**
20 to 25 **pepperoni slices,** halved
$^3/_4$ cup **chopped green bell pepper**
$^1/_2$ cup **grated cheddar cheese**
I cup **grated mozzarella cheese**

Preheat oven to 350 degrees.

Cook noodles in water according to package directions and drain.

In a saucepan, combine sauce, pepperoni, pepper, and cheddar cheese.
Stir constantly until cheese is melted.

Place noodles in a lightly greased 8 x 8-inch pan. Pour sauce mixture over
top. Sprinkle with mozzarella cheese. Bake 15 minutes, or until cheese is
melted. Makes 2–4 servings.

LASAGNA

2 packages **ramen noodles,** any flavor
2 cups **spaghetti sauce**
I cup **ricotta cheese**
I cup **grated mozzarella cheese**
I cup **Parmesan cheese**

Preheat oven to 350 degrees.

Cook noodles in water according to package directions and drain. Stir sauce into noodles.

In an 8 x 8-inch pan, layer half of the noodle mixture, ricotta, mozzarella, and Parmesan cheeses. Repeat layers. Bake 20 minutes. Makes 2–4 servings.

PRIMAVERA PASTA

$^1/_4$ cup **slivered almonds**
1 cup **chopped broccoli**
1 cup **snow peas**
1 cup **sliced red bell pepper**
$^1/_2$ cup **thinly sliced carrots**
$^1/_2$ cup **thinly sliced red onion**
3 tablespoons **vegetable oil**
2 packages **chicken ramen noodles,** broken up
1 $^1/_2$ cups **water**

In a frying pan, toast almonds until lightly browned and then set aside.
Stir-fry vegetables in oil 3–4 minutes. Add broken noodles and water.
Steam 3–5 minutes, or until noodles are done, stirring occasionally.
Top with almonds and serve. Makes 2–4 servings.

BEER NOODLES

2 tablespoons **vegetable oil**
1 package **ramen noodles,** any flavor, broken up
1 can (10.5 ounces) **onion soup,** condensed
1 soup can **beer**

Heat oil in a saucepan over medium heat. Add noodles and lightly
brown, stirring constantly. Add soup and beer. Cover and
simmer 10 minutes. Drain noodles and serve. Makes 2 servings.

PARMESAN NOODLES

2 packages **ramen noodles,** any flavor
$^1/_2$ cup **grated Parmesan cheese**
salt and pepper, to taste

Cook noodles in water according to package directions and drain. Add Parmesan to warm noodles and stir until cheese is melted. Sprinkle with more Parmesan cheese if desired. Season with salt and pepper. Makes 2–4 servings.

CHEESY RANCH RAMEN

2 packages **finely chopped ramen noodles,** any flavor
I cup **ranch dressing**
2 cups **grated cheddar cheese**

Cook noodles in water according to package directions and drain. Add ranch dressing and cheese to noodles and cook over low heat, stirring constantly, until cheese is melted. Makes 2–4 servings.

BUTTERY CHIVE NOODLES

2 packages **ramen noodles,** any flavor
2 tablespoons **butter** or **margarine**
$^1/_2$ cup **chopped chives**
salt and pepper, to taste

Cook noodles in water according to package directions and drain. Add butter to warm noodles and stir until melted. Add chives and season with salt and pepper. Makes 2–4 servings.

RAMEN TRAIL MIX

3 packages **ramen noodles,** any flavor
15 small sticks **beef jerky,** cut into small pieces
1/2 pound **dried apricots,** cut into small pieces*
1/2 cup **dried cranberries, blueberries, cherries,** or **bananas**
2 cups **dry roasted peanuts**

Break noodles into a bowl. Add remaining ingredients and stir. Makes 12 cups.

VARIATION: For a more traditional trail mix, omit the beef jerky and fruit. Add 1 pound plain M&Ms, 1 cup raisins, 1 cup sunflower seeds, and 3 cups granola cereal to broken up noodles and stir.

*Any dried fruit combination may be substituted.

RAMEN HAYSTACKS

2 cups	**butterscotch chips**
I tablespoon	**butter**
I tablespoon	**milk**
I package	**ramen noodles,** any flavor, crumbled

In a saucepan, heat butterscotch, butter, and milk over low heat until chips are completely melted. Stir crumbled, uncooked noodles into butterscotch mixture until coated. Place spoon-sized balls on wax paper, and refrigerate until cool. Makes 4–6 servings.

CHOCOLATE CHINOS

2 packages **ramen noodles,** any flavor
3 cups **milk chocolate chips**
2 cups **mini marshmallows**
$^1/_2$ cup **coconut**
$^1/_2$ cup **chopped walnuts**

Preheat oven to 350 degrees.

Do not break noodles. Put blocks of noodles in a lightly greased
8 x 8-inch pan. Cover with layers of chocolate chips and marshmallows.
Heat in warm oven until marshmallows and chocolate chips are melted.
Layer remaining ingredients over top and refrigerate. When cooled,
cut into bars. Makes 6–8 servings.

PEACH TREATS

I cup	**cream**
I small can	**peaches,** drain and reserve juice
$^1/_2$ cup	**peach juice** (from can)
$^1/_4$ cup	**brown sugar**
I package	**ramen noodles,** any flavor, crushed
$^1/_2$ cup	**crushed frosted flakes**

Preheat oven to 350 degrees.

In a small casserole dish, mix cream, peaches, peach juice, and brown sugar. Add crushed noodles, making sure they are completely covered by cream mixture. Bake 5 minutes. Sprinkle frosted flakes over top and bake 5 minutes more. Makes 2 servings.

MAPLE AND BROWN SUGAR RAMENMEAL

I package	**ramen noodles,** any flavor
I cup	**milk**
I tablespoon	**syrup**
I tablespoon	**brown sugar**

Crumble ramen into a microwave-safe bowl. Pour on milk, syrup, and sugar. Heat in the microwave on high 4 minutes, stirring occasionally. Makes 2 servings.

VARIATION: If you'd rather have something fruity, omit the syrup and sugar and add I banana, sliced, I cup of blueberries, or a mixture of I/2 diced apples, I teaspoon cinnamon, and I tablespoon sugar.

Vegetable
Entrees

BROCCOLI-CAULIFLOWER RAMEN

I can (10.75 ounces) **cream of celery soup,** condensed
$^1/_2$ cup **milk**
I cup **broccoli pieces**
$^1/_2$ cup **cauliflower pieces**
$^1/_2$ cup **sliced carrots**
I package **ramen noodles,** any flavor,
with seasoning packet

In a saucepan, heat soup and milk to boiling. Stir in vegetables and heat to boiling. Reduce heat and simmer 15 minutes.

Cook noodles in water according to package directions and drain. Add seasoning packet. Top warm noodles with soup mixture. Makes 2 servings.

CHEESY VEGETABLE RAMEN

I package	**ramen noodles,** any flavor, with seasoning packet
I cup	**frozen mixed vegetables**
I tablespoon	**water**
I small jar	**creamy cheese sauce,** condensed

Cook noodles in water according to package directions and drain. Add
$1/2$ of the seasoning packet and set aside.

In a frying pan, cook vegetables in water until tender. Add cheese sauce to
vegetables and heat through. Stir in noodles. Makes 2 servings.

HOLLANDAISE VEGETABLES

I package	**chicken ramen noodles,** with seasoning packet
2	**egg yolks**
3 tablespoons	**lemon juice**
$^1/_2$ cup	**butter** or **margarine,** divided
I cup	**fresh** or **frozen mixed vegetables**

Cook noodles in water according to package directions, and drain.

In a saucepan, whisk egg yolks and lemon juice briskly with a fork. Add $^1/_2$ of the butter and stir over low heat until melted. Add remaining butter, stirring briskly until melted and sauce thickens. Cook vegetables and drain. Top warm noodles with vegetables and sauce. Makes 2 servings.

VEGGIE SAUTE

I package	**ramen noodles,** any flavor, with seasoning packet
$^1/_2$ cup	**sliced onion**
$^1/_2$ cup	**diced tomato**
I can (4 ounces)	**mushrooms,** drained
$^1/_2$ cup	**chopped green bell pepper**
I teaspoon	**garlic powder**
2 tablespoons	**oil**

Cook noodles in water according to package directions and drain. Season noodles with $^1/_2$ of the seasoning packet.

In a frying pan, saute vegetables in garlic powder and oil over low heat until tender. Stir in warm noodles and serve. Makes 2 servings.

CHINESE FRIED NOODLES

2 packages	**Oriental ramen noodles,**
	with seasoning packets
I cup	**frozen peas and carrots**
2	**eggs**
I to 2 teaspoons	**oil**
2 to 3 tablespoons	**soy sauce**

Cook noodles in water according to package directions and drain. Add seasoning packets. Heat vegetables in microwave until heated through and add to warm noodles.

In a frying pan, fry eggs in oil; break yolk and cook until hard, flipping occasionally. Cut eggs into pieces. Stir into noodle mixture. Sprinkle soy sauce over top and stir together, adding more if necessary. Makes 2–4 servings.

TOMATO SAUTE

2 packages	**ramen noodles,** any flavor, with seasoning packets
1 cup	**butter** or **margarine**
2 cans (14.5 ounces each)	**diced tomatoes**
2 teaspoons	**minced garlic**

Cook noodles in water according to package directions and drain.

In a frying pan, melt butter. Add tomatoes, garlic, seasoning packets, and noodles and stir. Season with salt and pepper. Simmer 5 minutes. Makes 2–4 servings.

GARLIC CILANTRO NOODLES

2 packages **Oriental ramen noodles,** with seasoning packets
2 cups **fresh** or **frozen mixed vegetables**
1 teaspoon **minced garlic**
2 tablespoons **fresh chopped cilantro**

Cook noodles and vegetables in water together and drain. Add garlic, cilantro, and seasoning packets. Simmer over low heat 5 minutes, stirring occasionally. Makes 2–4 servings.

CHINESE VEGGIE NOODLES

I package **Oriental ramen noodles,** with seasoning packet
I cup **frozen stir-fry vegetables**
I $1/2$ teaspoons **olive oil**
I tablespoon **soy sauce**

Cook noodles in water according to package directions and drain. Add seasoning packet.

In a frying pan, saute vegetables in olive oil until heated through and add to warm noodles. Sprinkle soy sauce over top and stir together. Season with salt and pepper. Makes 2 servings.

CORNY CHEESE NOODLES

1 package **ramen noodles,** any flavor,
with seasoning packet
1 1/2 cups **grated cheddar cheese**
1 can (14 ounces) **creamed corn**

Cook noodles in water according to package directions and drain. Add seasoning packet.

In a saucepan, heat cheese and corn over medium heat. Mix with warm noodles. Makes 2 servings.

NOTES

NOTES

NOTES

NOTES

NOTES

NOTES

ABOUT THE AUTHOR

Toni Patrick, the culinary genius behind *101 Things to Do with Ramen Noodles,* created the book while she was a student at the University of Northern Colorado. She admits to not being a cook, but out of necessity can do "great things" with ramen noodles on a limited budget.

Toni was once named Irreverent Person of the Year by *Irreverent Magazine* for coming up with the idea of a ramen noodle cookbook while living in the shadow of Colorado's largest meat packing facility. She is now living deep in the Rocky Mountains with her dog, Buddy, and two cats Jiminy and Cricket. Toni enjoys playing in the snow, ice fishing, and curling up by the fire with a good book.